SEE NO GENDER

Abhijit Naskar is the twenty-first century mind of science, whose seminal philosophical touch has enabled modern Neuroscience to effectively engage in the human society towards diminishing the ever-growing conflicts among religions. As an untiring advocate of global harmony and peace, he became a beloved best-selling author all over the world with his very first book "The Art of Neuroscience in Everything". With various of his pioneering ventures into the Neuropsychology of religious sentiments, he has hugely contributed in the eradication of religious differences in our world, for which he is popularly hailed as a humanitarian neuroscientist, who takes the human civilization in the path of sweet general harmony.

See No
GENDER

ABHIJIT NASKAR

Also by Abhijit Naskar

The Art of Neuroscience in Everything
Your Own Neuron: A Tour of Your Psychic Brain
The God Parasite: Revelation of Neuroscience
The Spirituality Engine
Love Sutra: The Neuroscientific Manual of Love
Homo: A Brief History of Consciousness
Neurosutra: The Abhijit Naskar Collection
Autobiography of God: Biopsy of A Cognitive Reality
Biopsy of Religions: Neuroanalysis towards Universal
Tolerance
Prescription: Treating India's Soul
What is Mind?
In Search of Divinity: Journey to The Kingdom of Conscience
Love, God & Neurons: Memoir of a scientist who found
himself by getting lost
The Islamophobic Civilization: Voyage of Acceptance
Neurons of Jesus: Mind of A Teacher, Spouse & Thinker
Neurons, Oxygen & Nanak
The Education Decree
Principia Humanitas
The Krishna Cancer
Rowdy Buddha: The First Sapiens
We Are All Black: A Treatise on Racism
The Bengal Tigress: A Treatise on Gender Equality
Either Civilized or Phobic: A Treatise on Homosexuality
Wise Mating: A Treatise on Monogamy
Illusion of Religion: A Treatise on Religious
Fundamentalism
The Film Testament
Human Making is Our Mission: A Treatise on Parenting
I Am The Thread: My Mission
7 Billion Gods: Humans Above All
Lord is My Sheep: Gospel of Human
Morality Absolute
A Push in Perception
Let The Poor Be Your God
Conscience over Nonsense
Saint of The Sapiens
Time to Save Medicine
Fabric of Humanity

Build Bridges not Walls: In the name of Americana
The Constitution of The United Peoples of Earth
Lives to Serve Before I Sleep
When Humans Unite: Making A World Without Borders
All For Acceptance
Monk Meets World
Mission Reality
Citizens of Peace: Beyond The Savagery of Sovereignty
Operation Justice

To Leah,
My Doc Unstoppable

The world is full of doctors,
but healers are rare.
The world is full of pills,
but medicine is rare.
The world is full of stethoscopes,
but listening is rare.
And when someone's in misery,
I have no doubt you'll appear.

CONTENTS

Step Beyond Feminism

Gender equality – it is not simply a phrase – it is hope – it is dignity – it is equality – it is humanity. Without this simple yet most magnificent characteristic, a species is not even entitled to call itself either civilized or even sapient for that matter, because sapient means wise, and a species can be hailed as wise, only if it has equality flowing through its veins.

However, we must not confuse gender equality with the term feminism. Gender equality and feminism are not the same thing. Gender equality is a fundamental characteristic of a civilized and progressive society, whereas feminism is an ideological path that attempts to instill that quality in the society.

And indeed, feminism appeared as a viable means - as an empowering humanitarian movement in an uncompromisingly patriarchal society during the 19th and early 20th century. It made the society think - it made the society question its predominant norms that either consciously or subconsciously undermined feminine value and promoted masculine superiority. And as such, feminism can never be seen as a toxic phenomenon - if anything, it is one of the most progressive phenomena of human history.

Let's move very slow here and try to understand with all our attention – our undivided, non-conflicted attention. Can you do that my friend? Can you give that attention?

If we really look at the matter of feminism, from a naïve, uninfluenced perspective, then we can realize that the feminist movement is not much different from another movement that you would be very much aware of – it is the pride movement.

Think about it a little. Take a pause. Now ask yourself – isn't the pride movement similar to the feminist movement, in its struggle for equality – in its struggle for the fundamental rights of human beings!

Now let's ask an elementary question. What caused the feminist movement? And that answer is oppression – it is discrimination. However, every movement has both positive and negative sides.

Because every movement is the product of collective human actions – and the humans themselves are a collection of good and bad elements – positive and negative elements – civilized and uncivilized elements – human and inhuman elements – conscientious and barbarian elements. As such, anything that the humans do or create most inadvertently has some elements from both sides, good and bad. The same is true for the feminist movement.

Although, in theory, feminism is predicated primarily on the idea that women should be given the same rights as men, in practice, it is not as simple as that. So, let's investigate what's wrong with feminism and what's right with feminism. But again, if you are aggravated by the very possibility that there could be something wrong with feminism, then you should stop reading right away, for blindness towards the negative aspects of one's belief is the biggest impediment to knowledge.

We can continue only if you are genuinely interested in investigating, without any preconceived conclusions on the matter. Usually there are two kinds of people - those who support feminism and those who are against feminism. Here, both these people see the movement through the tainted glasses of their biased and limited perception.

One recognizes the anguish of the women – hence they see the need for the movement and the other sees the hateful outbursts of some feminists – they see the negative side of women –they see the angry side of women – hence they hate the movement altogether. But the truth, as usual, is beyond this duality.

Women have been suppressed for too long – society has been created by men – that's why it's a patriarchal society. But it's only recently that the society has been considering of giving women the same rights as they give the men, because they feel the need for it – they are beginning to find the discrimination to be unfounded. So, a huge portion of the society feels the need for seeing women finally as human beings, and not as inferior beings to men.

However, the interesting part is, women have been suppressed for so long, that psychologically they have become biased against themselves as well – biased against their own gender, without even being aware of it. So, the bias in gender is not an exclusive phenomenon among the men – it is in woman as well. Women are biased against women.

Now here please observe the matter without seeing yourself as a man or woman or anything else – only then you can perceive the phenomenon with all its roots, nuances and implications. I beg you not to jump to conclusion. We are not here to conclude or judge – we are here to understand the phenomenon of feminist movement.

After a long struggle against themselves and the society, finally women are starting to realize their potential. The need for rights, the need for equality, made women feel the oppression and now they have finally mustered the power to stand up to the oppression. Hence arose feminism. And now women as well as men are speaking up for equality and against discrimination.

There are two portions of the movement – one portion consists of the women who really want equality, and who themselves would never in a million years support any kind of hatred and discrimination against men. They are conscious enough to not let their advocacy of gender equality turn into hatred and prejudice. These women try their best to not turn into the same kind of gender biased people they have had to face their whole life.

Now, there is another portion of the movement that consists of women who are so much driven by their hostility against the society – against the patriarchal oppression of the society, that the rational parts of their psyche get overwhelmed by avenging emotions. Hence, they are driven not by conscience or civilized behavior or a conscientious vision for peace and rights, but by the primitive sentimental force of revenge. They are driven by hatred and anger against the patriarchy, against men – which leads to the harmful side of the feminist movement.

In short, there are conscientious women, there are primitive women – there are conscientious men, there are primitive men – there are conscientious doctors, there are primitive doctors – there are conscientious scientists, there are primitive scientists – there are conscientious teachers, there are primitive teachers – there are conscientious preachers, there are primitive preachers – and so on.

The human mind has two facets – conscientious and primitive, or in simple terms, good and bad. We have them both in our psyche. It is biologically impossible to not have either one. So, it is not about possessing the primitive side or not possessing the primitive side. What makes us civilized is our awareness of the primitiveness within us, for with this awareness we can healthily modulate our behavior and try our best not to turn into hateful barbarians.

And this applies to every single human being on earth – and to every movement on earth. Every kind of movement against a regime – against a system – against a paradigm, inadvertently fosters a kind of hatred. In most cases that hatred is subconscious, but it's still there.

So, if we are not aware, these primitive elements – the elements of hate, rage, vengeance and so on, do have the power to turn us, who are fighting for equality, into the same kind of monstrosity we are fighting against. Awareness is the key. So, in short, there is nothing wrong in supporting the feminist movement – there is nothing wrong in supporting a movement that advocates for equality and rights. In fact, if you do not support equal rights – if you do not stand against discrimination – if you do not speak up against oppression - then you are not even qualified to be called a human.

Because a human is the one who is a human above all labels – who is a human above all discriminations – who is a human above all prejudices. And the feminist movement has such humans on its side indeed, but it also has the vengeful inhumans, who are as dangerous as religious extremists.

Hence it is the responsibility of all humans to empower and strengthen the positive elements of the human psyche – the elements of civilized behavior – so that, the discriminated do need to take shelter under an ideology. It is the responsibility of all humans to encourage and empowerment conscientious actions against all sorts of discrimination, both in ourselves and in others. This is our uncompromisable responsibility – the responsibility of every single human being.

And if you can realize this responsibility, then there will no longer be any need for the society to take refuge under any specific ism, for your every action will bring out the best of all isms in the society, without all the biases that come along in the path of loyalty towards a specific ism.

The point is, creating an actual gender neutral society, is not the work of an immature, greedy and materially obsessed species - it is the work of a conscientious, self-regulated and humane species - and we are far from it - we are a species under construction - and the first step to progress is to accept this simple fact of organic human existence.

We are not a perfect species - in fact, the very notion of perfection is the illusive mental construct of a juvenile species. There is no such thing as perfection, for nature is only nature - it's beyond our petty measures of perfection and imperfection. And once you realize this in your bones, you would attain an inexplicable sense of freedom - freedom from the urge to get to somewhere - freedom from the craving to become perfect - freedom from the dependency on social approval and appraisal.

Only with freedom can we build a society with equality as the backbone and conscience as the nerve center. Such a society would not be dependent on any ideology or school of thought, yet it won't be hesitant to learn the good from all the ideologies and schools of thought that the world has to offer, no matter their cultural background and origin. When learning stops, progress stops - when learning begins, with it begins progress. So, unless you want to end up as a medieval baboon, never stop learning, no matter your age, race or religion.

When one stops learning, one becomes ridiculously blind to the biases in one's beliefs. Having a different belief system is not a crime, but having a belief system that belittles other belief systems, is not just a crime, but downright dangerous to peace and progress. It's a crime against humanity, even if the law is yet to accept it as such, in the name of free speech. Extremism is injurious to peace. Extremism is injurious harmony. Extremism is injurious to progress.

Now, here we must investigate the very nature of the term extremism in order to understand it better. Although the society has been conditioned through various mediums, especially through television media, to automatically associate the term extremism with religion, it is not exclusive to religion. Extremism is a basic human drive, which can act either as a positive motivator for good or as a devastating fuel for disharmony.

But when you hear the term extremist, you probably think of violence and bloodshed. And that's because, the media has used the term "extremism" in explaining acts of religious terrorism for so long, that the minds of the masses have become conditioned to automatically associate extremism with religious terrorism. But the term extremism itself is neither kind nor cruel.

Being an extremist doesn't mean harming others for the benefit of one's cause - rather it means, even the annihilation of oneself for a cause seems insignificant. It depends on the nature of the cause, whether the extremism for that cause will cause death and destruction, or will it create a humane, just and loving society.

For example, I am an extremist - an extremist for peace - an extremist for harmony - an extremist for acceptance - even to the point of being masochistic - even to the point of being threatened by religious extremists. I would rather die as an extremist of acceptance and harmony, than give in to the extremists of segregation and disharmony.

These extremists of segregation and disharmony do not necessarily have to be religious extremists, they can be atheist extremists, nationalist extremists, feminist extremists and so on. In short, if a person strongly believes in an ideology, and is ready to go to extreme lengths to defend the supremacy of that specific ideology over all else, then that person is practically an extremist, in the traditional sense of the term.

And the trouble begins when an ideology becomes more important in the eyes of its followers than human life. If a community of people is in distress, then a human should do everything in his or her power to uplift their condition, not in the name of an ideology, but in the name of plain ordinary humanity. For humanity's sake, one must never entertain any sort of extremism, in the traditional ideological sense of the term. Obedience to an ideology leads to a fragmented mind and a fragmented mind leads to a broken society.

But the point is, in a civilized society, we cannot get rid of extremist aggression with counter aggression, because by doing so, we would be stooping to the same primitive level as that of the extremists. So, what is the way out of this extremist obsession of a portion of the human population, one wonders! The legal way would be to ban all sorts of extremist activity. But to do that, the human society must wake up themselves from their sleep of indifference. Only when the people are awake, can the policymakers feel the urgency to act upon the responsibility to eliminate extremism through legislation. In a progressive and humane society, legislation must be compatible with human rights - human rights must be compatible with reasoning - and reasoning must be compatible with evidence.

Such a society would not need the shelter of feminism to speak up for the rights of women, for speaking up for the rights of every human would be the fundamental characteristic of every conscientious human in that society.

The point is, contrary to our traditional ancestral belief, women are not socially less capable than men, in fact, in many aspects, women are more capable of maintaining progress and harmony in the society than men are, but for civilization's sake, all genders must work together without belittling each other if we are to live in a humane and mentally rejuvenating society.

Women deal with internal conflicts on a monthly basis, and as such, conflict resolution is their special forte, whereas men's special forte is fighting to win a conflict. So, it stands to reason that women can create a more harmonious society than men. However, such would still be an inhuman society, because absolute supremacy of women in social matters will make the men feel unworthy, insecure and deprived, even if they have all the comfort in the world, which will in time lead to yet another social revolt.

It's not about comfort - it's about having a say in the matters of one's society. So, to have a genuinely humane and healthy society, it is imperative that all humans are involved in the making of the society. Remember, it's not the most advanced society we should be aiming to build that only cares for efficiency, rather our aim should be to build a healthy society with the right amount of advancement and a whole lot of humaneness.

Binary Gender Dynamics

See no gender, hear no gender, speak no gender - see only human, hear only human, speak only human. This does not mean that gender has no role to play in the society. This does not mean that men and women feel, think and behave the same way.

Let me make it very clear and unambiguous. Men and women do not feel, think and behave the same way - they have their own distinct and unique mental universes, but the most important fact to be aware of here is that, no gender is inferior to another. They are not the same, they are different, but one is neither inferior nor superior to another. Now let's dive deep into the actual neuropsychological dynamics of men and women.

The male and female brains are wired differently. For this reason, the male brain perceives every situation of daily life from a typically male perspective and expects the female to do the same, while the female brain observes everything in a feminine manner and expects the male to do the same. And from this very difference emerge all the conflicts between the feminine and masculine opposites of the society.

The way of life in the wild conditioned the male and female brain to develop certain gender specific dominant characteristics. This gender difference in cognitive and behavioral characteristics is what we call sexual dimorphism. These sexually dimorphic neurobiological traits create a person's personality as well as the personality of an entire society, for a society begins with a person. So, to understand the society, we must understand the person – the individual.

Let's take the phenomenon of gut feeling or intuition for example. Whether you call it "gut-feeling" or "intuition", it technically is mind-reading. And biologically speaking, women are better at this than men. There is a fascinating interplay of brain circuits behind this phenomenon of gut-feeling.

Gut feelings are not just free-floating emotional states but actual physical sensations that convey meaning to certain areas in the brain. And studies have shown that the areas of the brain that are involved in gut feelings are larger and more sensitive in the female brain than the male brain.

At first a woman begins receiving emotional signals from another person's facial expressions, hand gestures, body postures and breathing rates through firing of the mirror neurons. And there is no mysticism involved in it. It's just simple yet beautiful biological design evolved through the process of natural selection.

Brain-scan studies have shown that the simple act of observing another person in a particular emotional state can automatically trigger similar brain region activity in the observer by the grace of the Mirror Neuron System (MNS), this is what we call "emotional empathy". And females are especially good at this kind of emotional mirroring.

Mirror neurons were first found in various regions of the monkey brain (Macaca nemestrina and Macaca mulatta). So far scientists have observed the wonderful neurons in areas like the ventral premotor cortex (vPMC), inferior parietal lobe (IPL), primary motor cortex and dorsal premotor cortex (dPMC).

Originally it was discovered, that the mirror neurons (MN) discharge both when the monkey does a particular action and when it observes another individual (monkey or human) doing a similar action. The name itself implies the significant feature of MNs. This specific feature of 'mirroring' or more specifically 'imitating' has been evolutionarily crucial in shaping the modern human civilization.

Studies have demonstrated quite extensively that when humans observe an action done by another individual their motor cortex becomes active even without the presence of any motor activity. The Mirror Neuron System has vast impact over a person's social and behavioral skills throughout the lifetime. It allows us to be human and understand another human being and even other species for that matter. When you see a person get beaten up in the park, you suddenly start to feel his agony. The same happens when you see a street dog getting hurt. Humans are biologically designed to actually feel another creature's pain, happiness and desires, as if it is our own pain, happiness and desires.

After the mirror neurons play their part, the body sends a message to the insula and anterior cingulate cortex of the brain. The insula is an area in a classic part of the brain where gut feelings are first processed. The anterior cingulate cortex, which is larger and more easily activated in females than males, is a critical area for anticipating, judging, controlling, and integrating negative emotions. A woman's pulse rate suddenly bumps up, a feeling of tension felt in her belly and the brain interprets it as an intense emotion.

So, being able to guess what another person is thinking or feeling is technically very much biological. And overall, between the male and female, the female brain is efficient at assessing the thoughts, beliefs and intentions of others, based on the smallest hints more quickly than the male brain. Such unique feature in the female brain is yet another product of evolutionary practice, as throughout evolutionary history a woman had to be very receptive of the facial expressions of her child, in order to ensure its well-being.

In the male brain, most emotions trigger less gut sensation and more rational thought. The typical male brain reaction to an emotion is to avoid it at all costs and find a rational solution to the problem. I remember, one of my colleagues once asked her scientist husband *"Why do men respond to emotional issues with logic instead of feelings?"* He laughed and said, *"The real question is why women don't."*

However, the mirror neurons of a man do allow him to briefly feel the same emotional pain he sees on a person's face. Next, the temporo-parietal junction activates his brain's analytical circuits to search his entire brain for solutions. This is called "cognitive empathy". The male brain is able to use the temporo-parietal junction starting in late childhood, and after puberty a man's reproductive hormones reinforce the preference for it. Researchers have found that the temporo-parietal junction keeps a firm boundary between emotions of the "self" and the "other". This prevents men's thought processes from being influenced by other people's emotional weakness, which strengthens their ability to cognitively and analytically find a solution without being vulnerable.

For example, many women in relationship often complain that their men are blind to the emotional signals they send. That's not actually the men's fault. While the female brain is a high-performance emotion engine, the male brain is not so skilled at reading facial expressions and emotional innuendoes, like signs of despair and hopelessness. Men pick up the subtle signs of sadness in a female face only 40 percent of the time, whereas women can pick up these signs 90 percent of the time. The only way to penetrate their shell of logical thinking, is to burst into tears. It's only when men actually see tears, they realize, that something's wrong. That's why women have evolved to cry four times more easily than men by displaying an unambiguous sign of suffering that men can't ignore.

One of the beautiful innate qualities of female psyche is to be there for her loved ones during emotionally difficult times. Women are neurologically wired to respond to the distress of other people quite instantly. So when men say "women blow things out of proportion", what they don't realize is that the male brain is a high-performance logicality machine, while on the other hand the woman's brain is neurologically programmed by Mother Nature to be more sensitive to emotional distress.

Researchers at the University of Michigan have discovered that women use both sides of the brain to respond to emotional experiences, while men use just one side. The left hemisphere is strongly involved in the sense of self, whereas the right hemisphere is responsible for the awareness of others.

Studies have also shown that the connections between the emotion centers in women are more active and extensive than men. In another study, at Stanford University, volunteers looked at emotional images while having their brains scanned. Nine different brain areas lit up in women, while in men only two lit up. No wonder, a woman always sticks around when a loved one is hurt or disturbed and would do everything in her capacity to make him or her feel comfortable.

While on the contrary men tend to avoid contact with emotionally distressed people. Men tend to process their troubles alone and expect women would do the same, which is just the opposite of what women expect. It's all about biological design. Also, research has also shown that women remember emotional events such as first dates, vacations and big arguments more vividly and retain them longer than men.

In the human brain an almond shaped structure located deep within the brain called the amygdala is the emotional coordinating system. From the amygdala emotional impulses go to the hypothalamus (the brain's Homeostasis center). Then the hypothalamus raises the blood pressure, heart rate and breathing, and puts the body into fight-or-flight mode based on the intensity of the emotional impulses. The amygdala also alerts the cortex (the brain's Intelligence center) which analyses the emotional situation and decides how much attention is required. If the intensity of the emotional impulses is high enough then the conscious brain becomes alert and strong conscious emotional sensation kicks in. Then the prefrontal cortex (the brain's decision-making center) plays its part by determining how to respond to the situation.

Women are way better at recollecting minuscule details of the emotional events of life. One reason for this is their highly sensitive amygdala, which is more easily activated by emotional triggers than in men. The amygdala's neural connections to the rest of the brain put it in a unique position to rapidly respond to sensory input and influence physiological and behavioral responses, as well as to influence memory formation in the adjacent hippocampus.

The stronger our amygdala responds to an emotional situation, the more details of that situation are indexed by the hippocampus. The hippocampus is the brain's memory formation center. It connects minute emotional senses like smell, sound etc. to memories and sends the memories out to the appropriate part of the cerebral hemisphere for long-term storage.

It's really very simple. The more emotional you are in a situation, the more memories you'll have of that situation in the long run. In this context, one thing to mention is that, sexual dimorphism in the hippocampal volume has also been found in many studies. Or in simple terms, the very memory indexer of the brain is actually larger in women than men.

So, when a man cannot remember the details about the first date, it doesn't at all mean that he does not love his woman any more. It's simply because his brain circuits are unable to retain the information. Men's amygdala and hippocampus work at full throttle in response to any threat to a relationship or any physical danger. In terms of emotional memories, men register memories connected to any kind of threatening situation as vividly as women register all emotional memories. To a man any threat to a relationship can be devastating which he never forgets.

The most innate biological response of men is aggression. It's an irrefutable part of the male existence. And the expression of rage and aggression is greater in men. The cause of men's anger and aggression is their larger amygdala and loads of testosterone receptors in it.

In an adult human brain, the male amygdala is significantly larger than the female amygdala, even when total brain size is taken into consideration. While on the contrary women have slightly larger prefrontal cortex and anterior cingulate cortex that are involved in controlling the rage and avoiding any kind of conflict. As a result women have better hold of their anger response than men.

The female brain is engineered to avoid conflicts at all cost, whereas the male brain pleasures conflicts in the purpose of being the boss. Studies have found that though men and women say that they feel anger for an equal number of minutes per day, men get physically aggressive twenty times more often than women. Due to the abundance of testosterone receptors in the amygdala, high testosterone level makes it even more difficult for a man to tame his rage and aggression.

Other than testosterone a man's brain circuit for aggression is highly influenced by vasopressin, cortisol and adrenalin. And actually in most cases when a man's anger reaches the boiling point it gives him an utter sensation of pleasure. The pleasure of utter aggression motivates a man to win a fight with more zeal.

All of these gender specific cognitive and behavioral traits are evolutionarily encoded inside the human brain to serve only one purpose and that is, survival of the species. However, they evolved mostly under the influence of a life in the wild, but now that lifestyle has changed – and along with it should change our cognitive and behavioral traits.

And the point is, no other species than the humans have the brain capacity to actually influence the neural wirings of their own mental and behavioral processes. For the first time in the history of life on earth, we the humans have developed the cognitive capacity to drive the process of our own biological evolution in a direction of our choosing at our own conscious will. So, choose wisely my sisters and brothers.

35

Vision of Civilization

We can naively and rather foolishly proclaim that men and women are the same, by turning blind to the sexual dimorphism of the human psyche, but that won't help us solve the issues of our society caused by the dominance of one gender over another. To solve a problem we must first open our eyes to the facts.

Facts are one of the fundamental ingredients of a progressive and civilized society. Ignoring facts just because they are not compatible with our beliefs, leads to a prejudiced society. So, to have a practical understanding of reality, it is imperative to recognize and accept facts. And this naturally implies that one has to keep modifying one's perception of the world constantly with the discovery of new facts or evidence.

Let me elaborate. There was a time when people believed that the light that we see in the day sky comes from a deity called "Ra" – the Sun God. But with the arrival of evidence – with the arrival of facts, we got rid of such imaginative ideas – ideas that our ancestors came up with due to lack of evidence – due to lack of understanding. They hailed all nature to be possessed by some form of supernatural force.

They feared every single natural manifestation of power, like thunderstorms, droughts, rain, floods, earthquakes, landslides, volcanoes, fire, heat, and cold etc. To avoid intellectual effort they had to incorporate supernatural explanations to those phenomena. They basically suspected that all those natural events were the gods' way of showing that they were angry with our ancestors. Naturally, our primitive ancestors felt the urge to appease that anger by worshipping nature.

They started to worship all the elements of Mother Nature like stones, hills, trees, lakes, animals and many more as some deity or supernatural force. They believed that souls or spirits exist, not only in humans, but also in inanimate objects such as plants, rocks, mountains, rivers and other entities of the natural environment.

But we have come a long way since then. Now people in general no longer hold such supernatural beliefs about the elements of nature at least. Most of the human population has become mature enough in their psyche to accept the basic facts of the world we live in. Most people now know that the sun is simply a star in the sky giving light and not some luminous deity riding his chariot. Likewise, unlike our ancestors, today's humanity now accepts the fact that the earth is not the center of the universe.

In the same way, as we embarked on an investigation of life, we began to realize the futility of our ancestral notion that lifeforce comes from an external extraterrestrial kingdom into the body and when the body dies it goes back to that kingdom. Our investigation of life and biology brought forth the evidence that made it clear that life is born of organic matter – of biology.

When an organism is intact, healthy and capable of healing itself, it has life. But the moment the organism begins to malfunction and is no longer capable of healing itself, i.e. no longer capable of regenerating its cells, either due to an incurable disease or aging, that's the time it dies. And as a part of life, consciousness or to a broader aspect mind is also a product of protoplasmic activity.

The point is, if we are to move forward in the path of understanding – in the path of knowledge – in the path of truth – we must accept certain facts as they come to light. We cannot simply ignore the facts, just because they are not compatible with our beliefs – the beliefs that we are used to – just because they are not compatible with the traditions that we have been following for centuries or millennia.

We can call ourselves human only if we have the guts to accept our ignorance – to accept the mistakes of our past – to accept the arrogance of our ancestors, of our tradition, of our culture – to accept the harms of the egotism that has been passed on to us by our environment.

We can only call ourselves human, if we are ready to discard the beliefs that do not aid in constructing a society that's humane and inclusive – a society that has the force of reason in its veins – a society that is progressive and ready to learn even if it means discarding its most beloved beliefs.

But do not confuse facts to be the only fundamental ingredients of progress. Without a humane vision facts alone will create a mechanical society, on the other hand, without facts, sheer sentiments will create an unstable society. So, to create a healthy, stable, inclusive and progressive society, facts must be guided by a humane vision of the future.

And here I am not talking about imagination - I am talking about vision - such vision that appears more real than reality - a vision that doesn't allow you to sleep and rest. It's not some fleeting thought or desire or urge or ambition - it's a life-long madness - it's a mania - it's an obsession - an illumination - an illumination of the path ahead - a path that is invisible to everybody else but you - a path that if described to the majority, will only bring in mockery and ridicule, until they actually see the fruits of your toil manifesting as reality.

Some may say this is merely wishful thinking. And let me make it very clear - it is indeed wishful thinking, but an imperative wishful thinking. And when enough individuals sacrifice their soul for that one wishful thinking, sooner or later it is bound to turn into reality. But that's not even the primary factor to be aware of here - what is, is the fact that without the sacrifice of these braveheart individuals for a simple apparently wishful thought, our world will never become truly civilized and sapient. These apparently insane individuals are the forerunners of progress.

So ask yourself this simple question – are you insane enough for any such wishful thinking – for an idea! If you are, then no paradigm is big enough to depict your vision. Therefore, instead of trying to define your vision to others, you simply need to stand up and sacrifice all for that one idea - in your sacrifice, lies the elixir of progress. And remember, those who help humanity reap the fruits of progress by sowing the seeds with their own two hands, must do so knowing that they may never taste the fruits themselves.

World Beyond Gender

Some gender norms are healthy, some are unhealthy - you must wake up from the patriarchal sleep to recognize which is which. Replacing one discriminatory and oppressive system with another, doesn't solve the societal issues born from discrimination, it only makes them switch sides. Retaliating oppression with oppression only breeds more oppression, injustice and inequality, not rights, justice and equality.

And as I have said in one of my previous works:

"Even though the term "feminism" is founded upon the basic principle of gender equality, it possesses its own fundamental gender bias, which makes it inclined towards the wellbeing of women, over the wellbeing of the whole society. And if history has shown anything, it is that such fundamental biases in time corrupt even the most glorious ideas and give birth to prejudice, bigotry and differentiation."

To build a truly just and humane society with equal rights for every human, no one gender-based paradigm can take us far. We may begin the journey holding the bold and empowering hands of feminism, but along the way, we must let go off those hands and walk free and conscientious with our attention focused on human rights, instead of women's rights or men's rights.

Human is not just a word - it's a symbol - a symbol of hope - a symbol of compassion - a symbol of justice - a symbol of unity. Taking it for granted would mean losing the existential grandeur of human life. It's time that we teach humanity to the humans, and the only way to do that, is by being the emblem of humanity ourselves. And being an emblem of humanity means being an emblem of justice, equality, reasoning and acceptance.

When justice roars, injustice is bound to fade away. Roar for justice - roar for equality - roar for humanity - roar so loud with acts of conscience that all inhumanity crumbles to dust. One person can make a difference, but only if the person acts like a person, and not as an insect.

What is a person? Wearing clean clothes, eating good food and talking smart, do not make a creature a person - a person is one whose conscience is clean, bold and functional - a person is one whose mind is full with courage and compassion - a person is one who acts wise, instead of boasting with words of shallow smartness. Shred all pomp and ceremony of external sophistication and be a person from within – be a human – be humane.

Path of Humaneness

Humaneness is above all - it's above culture - it's above tradition - it's above heritage. This doesn't mean looking down on your cultural background, or trying to wipe it out altogether, rather it simply means, even though some of your cultural tenets and traditions may be alive in you, they, in no circumstances could outweigh your sense of humanity.

To see people as more important than traditions, beliefs and disbeliefs, is what turns an animal into a human. Stand free and stand human, and the whole world will stand by you. Tolerate no discrimination and moderate no compassion. Wild animals pay attention to caste and creed, humans pay attention to humanity. But this is easier said than done, especially because, our brain is more wired to follow the herd, than to think, feel and behave completely on its own, as an individual.

Our evolutionary drive for survival has conditioned us to be vulnerable to social priming or as you like to call it, social programming. Except for individuals with pathological apathy towards the society, such as sociopaths, nobody is impervious to social conditioning. And this includes everyone - you, me, everyone. But let's move very slow here, for these are murky waters of inquiry.

We all are wired instinctually to crave for social approval, appreciation and acceptance, for which we are more inclined to live our lives according to our society's will and wishes, than to our own original inclinations. Naturally, when a person goes against the norms of the society, to achieve something unique or original, he or she has to face society's disproval and mockery on top of the obstacles that come in the path of his or her purpose.

And when I said, nobody is impervious to social conditioning, it meant that, even if an individual goes on an original path instead of following the crowd, every now and then the person would still feel the craving to be accepted by his or her society - so long as the person is a living, breathing human, he or she would still feel the urge to seek approval from the society. But that's not the problem. What matters here is that the person continues on his or her original path, despite receiving only disapproval and mockery from the society.

The most interesting fact here is that, if all humans followed the norms of the society word by word, there wouldn't be any progress in the world whatsoever. Progress takes place only and only because of the handful of "misfits" who make their own path and keep walking and working on that path trampling all obstacles, agonies and criticisms. Society progresses only because of the individuals who would rather die in the path of their mission, than give in to societal pressure. But this is no easy task, for no task of world building is ever easy.

The mission must turn bigger than the person for the person to turn the mission into reality. I had and have such a mission - a mission to unify all of humankind. This mission turned a naïve college dropout into an insignia of equality, inclusion and acceptance. And so long as there is life in my veins, I won't let no extremism, arrogance and bigotry tear apart my people - my humanity. I am not a person - I am a mission - a mission of unity - the mission of harmony - a mission of egalitarianism.

The point is, extremism and bigotry can come in any form, even though the so-called intellectuals and unscrupulous journalists of the media would like you to believe otherwise, for they themselves are blinded by their own biases and conditionings. These can come in the form of religious fundamentalism - they can come in the form of heartless intellectualism - they can come in the form of spiritualism - they can come in the form of feminism - they can even come in the form of humanism.

No matter what the theoretical definition of an "ism" is, when the "ism" takes preference over human life, it automatically raises walls among people. All isms lead to sectarianism - sometimes this sectarianism is conscious, but in most cases, it's subconscious, which means that the follower of a certain ism is not even aware of the differentiation that the person fosters in the mind and contributes to the society.

And such subconscious, that is, implicit differentiation is more dangerous than explicit differentiation, for explicit differentiation is easily noticeable, but implicit or subconscious differentiation is the bug that keeps feeding on the humane backbone of the human society from within, without drawing any attention of either the self or the society.

Most of the world's implicit differentiations come in the form of identities - be it religious identity, national identity, political identity, intellectual identity and so on. But amidst the overwhelming crowd of these superficial identities, the highest identity of humanness or humanity turns invisible or secondary. And in the absence of the identity of humanity, all other sophisticated identities are worthless - without humanity, all nationalities are worthless - all religions are worthless, all ideologies are worthless, all intellect is worthless.

And the identity of humanity is not just an identity, it's a force of nature - a force for good - a force for harmony - a force for upliftment. I am a force of nature, I don't have nationality. Does the Everest have nationality? Does the Amazon have nationality? Does the Grand Canyon have nationality? They all belong to the world. Likewise, no matter where I live, I belong to the world. And no matter where you live, you belong to the world. Every human belongs to the whole world, for that very universal belonging is what makes humanity human. We belong to the world, we belong to each other, beyond race, religion, gender and sexual orientation.

Humanity lies in non-differentiation. Humanity lies in non-sectarianism. Humanity lies in unification. This humanity, that is, the "human character" is not determined by race, religion, gender or sexual orientation. In fact, there is no greater sin, no greater blasphemy than distancing others from oneself, based on their gender, faith, color or sexual orientation.

For example, if you think homosexuality is a sin, then your very life is a sin. If you think homosexuality is disgusting, then your very mind is disgusting. If you think homosexuality is a disease, then your very existence is a disease.

And I am not going to let any brainless and heartless ape from the medieval times to look down on my sisters and brothers for being homosexual. I will not use active violence, but I won't let no bigot raise their poisonous fangs while I am standing on guard for the society - for my people - for my humankind - for their happiness - for their rights - for their life.

No doctrine is more valuable than human life - no scripture is more valuable than human life - no deity, prophet or god is more valuable than human life. If a god, deity or scripture commands that being in love with a person of the same gender is a sin, then such god, deity or scripture is more dangerous to the wellbeing and progress of the human civilization than a dog with rabies.

Life has only one color that matters - humanity has only one character that matters - world has only one religion that matters - and that color, that character, that religion is love. All colors, characters and religions can exist either as reflections of love, or not at all.

Everything is chemical reaction - love, hate, kindness, courage, character, rage, empathy, religion, god, everything. Everything that makes us who we are, is a chemical reaction. Everything that makes nature what it is, is a chemical reaction. In fact, the whole universe is a chemical reaction. So, fighting over minuscule matters of faith, intellect, nationality, gender, sexual orientation and so on, is not only petty, but not worth our time and energy.

Each one of us is here on earth for only a few scores, so it is imperative that we spend our lifeforce and lifetime in doing something productive, inclusive and humane, instead of wasting them on destructive, discriminatory and inhuman purposes. Each drop of human blood has the potential to either humanize the planet or dehumanize it - it has the potential to either hypnotize the planet or dehypnotize it.

Water has the potential to grow life even in the barren desert, and it also has the potential to flood an entire city destroying countless lives - fire has the potential to give heat in the freezing winter, and it also has the potential to burn an entire forest to ashes. Potential is neither good nor evil, it's our intention that makes the distinction.

Do you have the intention to change this world - forget about all the so-called rational advice about not wasting your time on trying to change the world. Forget reasoning on this one question. Just feel - feel the urge to change this world - feel it boiling in your blood - feel it rushing through your veins. Do you feel the madness for change - a madness that knows no reasoning, a madness that knows no practicality

- a madness that knows no intellectualism or anti-intellectualism - all it knows is that it must, not should, but must act to change this society into a safe, healthy and inclusive place for the humans to live in!

Each human is a nuclear furnace of potential. And when even a handful of these furnaces come to the aid of the society, then the society is bound to become a just, humane and progressive abode for existence. You are not the future of humanity, for you won't live long enough to see the future - what you are is the present of humanity, and your actions in the present will determine the present of future humanity - of our children and all the children yet to come. Therefore, we must rush to the aid of the helpless - we must rush to the aid of the discriminated - we must rush to the aid of the segregated - we must rush to the aid of the alienated.

And remember,

Not woman, not man, not the non-binary;

No gender is able enough to sustain progress and harmony.

To make sure that we grow and stand tall with dignity;

All humans, no matter the gender, must rise together with humanity.

Bibliography

Archer M., (2000), Being Human: The Problem of Agency. Cambridge University Press.

Archer M., (2003), Structure, Agency and the Internal Conversation. Cambridge University Press.

Adolphs R (2003) Cognitive neuroscience of human social behaviour. Nature Rev Neurosci 4: 165–178.

Adolphs R, Tranel D, Damasio AR (2003) Dissociable neural systems for recognizing emotions. Brain Cogn 52: 61–69.

Afton, A. D. (1985). Forced copulation as a reproductive strategy of male lesser scaup: A field test of some predictions. - Behaviour 92, p. 146-167.

Allison T, Puce A, McCarthy G. (2000) Social perception from visual cues: role of the STS region. Trends Cogn Sci 4: 267–278.

Andresen, Jensine, and Robert Forman, eds. Cognitive Models and Spiritual Maps. Bowling Green, Ohio: Imprint Academic, 2000.

Ashbrook, James, and Carol Albright. The Humanizing Brain: Where Religion and Neuroscience Meet. Cleveland, OH: Pilgrim Press, 1997.

Azari, Nina, Janpeter Nickel, Gilbert Wunderlich, Michael Niedeggen, Harald Hefter, Lutz Tellmann, Hans Herzog, Petra Stoerig, Dieter Birnbacher, and Rudiger Seitz. "Neural Correlates of Religious Experience." European Journal of Neuroscience 13, no. 8 (2001)

Agar, N. (2004). Liberal eugenics: In defence of human enhancement. London: Blackwell Publishing.

Alteheld, N., Roessler, G., Vobig, M., & Walter, R. (2004). The retina implant new approach to a visual prosthesis. Biomedizinische Technik, 49(4), 99–103.

Antal, A., Nitsche, M. A., Kincses, T. Z., Kruse, W., Hoffmann, K. P., & Paulus, W. (2004a). Facilitation of visuo-motor learning by transcranial direct current stimulation of the motor and extrastriate visual areas in humans. European Journal of Neuroscience, 19(10), 2888–2892.

Bhat Z, Kumar, S, Bhat H (2015) In vitro meat production. Challenges and benefits over conventional meat production. J Sci Food Agric 14: 241–248

Bernstein R. J., (1967), John Dewey. New York: Washington Square Press.

Bernstein R.J., (1971), Praxis and Action: Contemporary Philosophies of Human Activity. Philadelphia: University of Pennsylvania Press.

Bernstein R.J., (1976), The Restructuring Social and Political Thought.

Bernstein R.J., (1983), Beyond Relativism and Objectivism: Science, Hermeneutics, and Praxis. Philadelphia: University of Pennsylvania Press.

Bernstein R.J., (1986), Philosophical Profiles. Philadelphia: University of Pennsylvania Press.

Bernstein R.J., (1991), New Constellation. Cambridge: MIT Press.

Barash, D. P. (1977). Sociobiology of rape in mallards (Anas platyrhynchos): Responses of the mated male. - Science 197, p. 788-789.

Berger, J. (1986). Wild horses of the great basin: Social competition and population size. - The University of Chicago Press, Chicago.

Birkhead, T. R., Johnson, S. D. & Nettleship, D. N. (1985). Extra-pair matings and mate guarding in the common murre Uria aalge. - Anim. Behav. 33, p. 608-619.

Beauregard, Mario, and Vincent Paquette. "Neural Correlates of a Mystical Experience in Carmelite Nuns." Neuroscience Letters 405, no. 3 (2006)

Benson, Herbert. Timeless Healing: The Power and Biology of Belief. New York: Scribner, 1996

Bogen, J.E.(1995a), 'On the neurophysiology of consciousness: Part I. An overview', Consciousness and Cognition, 4.

Bogen, J.E. (1995b), 'On the neurophysiology of consciousness: Part II. Constraining the semantic problem', Consciousness and Cognition, 4.

Bremner, J. D., R. Soufer, et al. (2001). "Gender differences in cognitive and neural correlates of remembrance of emotional words." Psychopharmacol Bull 35 (3).

Brothers, L. (2002). The social brain: A project for integrating primate behavior and neurophysiology in a new domain. In J. T. Cacioppo et al. (Eds.), Foundations in neuroscience. Cambridge, MA: MIT Press.

Buss, D. D. (2003). Evolutionary Psychology: The New Science of Mind, 2nd ed. New York: Allyn & Bacon.

Buss, D. M. (1989). "Conflict between the sexes: Strategic interference and the evocation of anger and upset." J Pers Soc Psychol 56 (5).

Buss, D. M. (1995). "Psychological sex differences. Origins through sexual selection." Am Psychol 50 (3).

Buss, D. M. (2002). "Review: Human Mate Guarding." Neuro Endocrinol Lett 23 (Suppl 4).

Buss, D. M., and D. P. Schmitt (1993). "Sexual strategies theory: An evolutionary perspective on human mating." Psychol Rev 100 (2).

Blakemore SJ, Decety J (2001) From the perception of action to the understanding of intention. Nature Rev Neurosci 2: 561.

Bruce C, Desimone R, Gross CG (1981) Visual properties of neurons in a polysensory area in superior temporal sulcus of the macaque. J Neurophysiol 46: 369–384.

Buccino G, Vogt S, Ritzl A, Fink GR, Zilles K, Freund HJ, Rizzolatti G (2004) Neural circuits underlying imitation of hand actions: an event related fMRI study. Neuron 42: 323–34.

Colapietro V., (1988), "Human Agency: The Habits of Our Being."

Southern Journal of Philosophy, XXVI, 2, pp. 153-68.

Colapietro V., (1992), "Purpose, Power, and Agency." The Monist, 75, 4 (October) pp. 423-44.

Colapietro V., (2003), "Signs and their vicissitudes: Meanings in excess of consciousness and functionality." Logica, Dialogica, Ideologica, a cure di Susan Petrilli e Patrizia Calefato (Milano: Mimesis), pp. 221-36.

Colapietro V., (2004a), "C. S. Peirce's Reclamation of Teleology." Nature in American Philosophy, ed. Jean De Groot (Washington, D.C.: Catholic University Press of America), pp. 88-108.

Colapietro V., (2004b), "Portrait of a Historicist: An Alternative Reading of Peircean Semiotic." Semiotiche, 2/04 [maggio 2004], pp. 49-68.

Colapietro V., (2006), "Engaged Pluralism: Between Alterity and

Sociality." The Pragmatic Century: Conversations with Richard J. Bernstein (Albany, NY: SUNY Press), pp. 39-68.

Colapietro V., (2009), "Habit, Competence, and Purpose." Forthcoming in The Transactions of the Charles S. Peirce Society.

Calder AJ, Keane J, Manes F, Antoun N, Young AW (2000) Impaired recognition and experience of disgust following brain injury. Nature Neurosci 3: 1077–1078.

Carey DP, Perrett DI, Oram MW (1997) Recognizing, understanding and reproducing actions. In: Jeannerod M, Grafman J (eds) Handbook of neuropsychology. Vol. 11: Action and cognition. Elsevier, Amsterdam.

Carr L, Iacoboni M, Dubeau MC, Mazziotta JC, Lenzi GL (2003) Neural mechanisms of empathy in humans: a relay from neural systems for imitation to limbic areas. Proc Natl Acad Sci USA 100: 5497–5502.

Changeux JP, Ricoeur P (1998) La nature et la règle. Odile Jacob, Paris.

Cochin S, Barthelemy C, Roux S, Martineau J (1999) Observation and execution of movement: similarities demonstrated by quantified electroencephalograpy. Eur J Neurosci 11: 1839– 1842.

Chomsky Noam, (2017) Requiem for the American Dream

Chomsky Noam, (2016) Who Rules the World?

Chomsky Noam, (2010) How the World Works

Churchland, P.S. (1986), Neurophilosophy (Cambridge, MA: The MIT Press).

Churchland, P.S. & Ramachandran, V.S. (1993), 'Filling in: Why Dennett is wrong', in Dennett and His Critics: Demystifying Mind, ed. B. Dahlbom (Oxford: Blackwell Scientific Press).

Churchland, P.S., Ramachandran, V.S. & Sejnowski, T.J. (1994), 'A critique of pure vision', in Large- scale Neuronal Theories of the Brain, ed. C. Koch & J.L. Davis (Cambridge, MA: The MIT Press).

Crick, F. (1994), The Astonishing Hypothesis: The Scientific Search for the Soul (New York: Simon and Schuster).

Crick, F. (1996), 'Visual perception: rivalry and consciousness', Nature, 379.

Crick, F. & Koch, C. (1992), 'The problem of consciousness', Scientific American, 267.

Craig AD (2002) How do you feel? Interoception: the sense of the physiological condition of the body. Nature Rev Neurosci 3: 655–666.

Damasio, A (2003a) Looking for Spinoza. Harcourt Inc. Damasio A (2003b) Feeling of emotion and the self. Ann NY Acad Sci 1001: 253–261.

d'Aquili, Eugene. "Senses of Reality in Science and Religion." Zygon 17, no 4 (1982)

d'Aquili, Eugene. "The Biopsychological Determinants of Religious Ritual Behavior." Zygon 10, no. 1 (1975)

d'Aquili, Eugene. "The Myth-Ritual Complex: A Biogenetic Structural Analysis." Zygon 18, no. 3 (1983)

d'Aquili, Eugene, and Andrew Newberg. The Mystical Mind: Probing the Biology of Religious Experience. Minneapolis: Fortress Press, 1999.

Daly DD. 1958. Ictal affect. Am J Psychiatry.

Damasio, A. (1994) Descartes' Error: Emotion, Reason and the Human Brain. New York, Putnams.

Damasio, A. (1999) The Feeling of What Happens: Body, Emotion and the Making of Consciousness. London, Heinemann.

Darwin, C. (1859) On the Origin of Species by Means of Natural Selection. London, Murray.

Darwin, C. (1871) The Descent of Man and Selection in Relation to Sex. London, John Murray.

Darwin, C. (1872) The Expression of the Emotions in Man and Animals. London, John Murray; also published 1965, Chicago, University of Chicago Press.

Dawkins, M.S. (1987) Minding and mattering. In C. Blakemore and S. Greenfield (eds) Mindwaves. Oxford, Blackwell, 151-60.

Dawkins, R. (1976) The Selfish Gene. Oxford, Oxford University Press; a new edition, with additional material, was published in 1989.

Dawkins, R. (1986) The Blind Watchmaker. London, Longman.

Di Pellegrino G, Fadiga L, Fogassi L, Gallese V, Rizzolatti G (1992) Understanding motor events: A neurophysiological study. Exp Brain Res 91: 176–80.

Deikman, A.J. (2000) A functional approach to mysticism. Journal of Consciousness Studies 7(11-12), 75-91.

Delmonte, M.M. (1987) Personality and meditation. In M. West (ed.) The Psychology of Meditation. Oxford, Clarendon Press, 118-32.

Dennett, D.C. (1987) The Intentional Stance. Cambridge, MA, MIT Press.

Dennett, D.C. (1988) Quining qualia. In A.J. Marcel and E. Bisiach (eds)

Consciousness in Contemporary Science. Oxford, Oxford University Press, 42-77.

Dennett, D.C. (1991) Consciousness Explained. Boston, MA, and London, Little, Brown and Co.

Dennett, D.C. (1995a) Darwin's Dangerous Idea. London, Penguin.

Dennett, D.C. (1995b) The unimagined preposterousness of zombies. Journal of Consciousness Studies 2(4), 322-6.

Dennett, D.C. (1995c) Cog: steps towards consciousness in robots. In T. Metzinger (ed.) Conscious Experience. Thorverton, Devon, Imprint Academic, 471-87.

Dennett, D.C. (1995d) The path not taken. Behavioral and Brain Sciences 18, 252-3; commentary on N. Block, On a confusion about a function of consciousness. Behavioral and Brain Sciences 18, 227.

Dennett, D.C. (1996a) Facing backwards on the problem of consciousness. Journal of Consciousness Studies 3(1), 4-6.

Dennett, D.C. (1996b) Kinds of Minds: Towards an Understanding of Consciousness. London, Weidenfeld & Nicolson.

Dennett, D.C. (1997) An exchange with Daniel Dennett. In J. Searle (ed.) The Mystery of Consciousness. New York, New York Review of Books, 115-19.

Dennett, D.C. (1998) The myth of double transduction. In S.R. Hameroff, A.W. Kaszniak and A. C. Scott (eds) Toward a Science of Consciousness: The Second Tucson Discussions and Debates. Cambridge, MA, MIT Press, 97-107.

Dennett, D.C. (1998b) Brainchildren: Essays on Designing Minds. Cambridge, MA, MIT Press.

Dennett, D.C. (2001) The fantasy of first person science. Debate with D. Chalmers, Northwestern University, Evanston, IL, February 2001.

Dennett, D.C. (2003) Freedom Evolves. New York, Penguin.

Dennett, D.C. and Kinsbourne, M. (1992) Time and the observer: the where and when of consciousness in the brain. Behavioral and Brain Sciences 15, 183-247, including commentaries and authors' responses.

Dewey J., (1911 [1977]), "Epistemological Realism: The Alleged Ubiquity of the Knowledge Relation." Journal of Philosophy, VIII, 20 (September 28, 1911).

Dewhurst, Kenneth, and A. W. Beard. "Sudden Religious Conversions in Temporal Lobe Epilepsy." British Journal of Psychiatry 117 (1970)

Dewhurst K, Beard AW. Sudden religious conversions in temporal lobe epilepsy. 1970 Epilepsy Behav 2003

Devinsky O, Lai G. Spirituality and religion in epilepsy. Epilepsy Behav 2008.

Devinsky, O., Morrell, MJ, Vogt, BA. (1995) 'Contribution of anterior cingulate cortex to behavior', Brain, 118.

E. Horvitz, "One Hundred Year Study on Artificial Intelligence: Reflections and Framing," ed: Stanford University, 2014.

Eckhart Meister, Selected Writings

Egidi R., ed. (1999), "Von Wright and 'Dante's Dream': Stages in a Philosophical Pilgrim's Progress", in In Search of a New Humanism: the Philosophy of G.H. von Wright, ed. by R. Egidi, Kluwer, Dordrecht.

Fadiga L, Fogassi L, Pavesi G, Rizzolatti G (1995) Motor facilitation during action observation: a magnetic stimulation study. J Neurophysiol 73: 2608–2611.

Fogassi L, Gallese V, Fadiga L, Rizzolatti G (1998) Neurons responding to the sight of goal directed hand/arm actions in the parietal area PF (7b) of the macaque monkey. Soc Neurosci Abs 24:257.5.

Frith U, Frith CD (2003) Development and neurophysiology of mentalizing. Philos Trans R Soc Lond B Biol Sci 358: 459.

Farah, M.J. (1989), 'The neural basis of mental imagery', Trends in Neurosciences, 10.

Finlay BL, Darlington RB (1995) Linked regularities in the development and evolution of mammalian brains. Science 268.

Freud, S. "The Interpretation of Dreams", 1900

Freud, S. "Selected papers on hysteria and other psychoneuroses" Journal of Nervous and Mental Disease 1909.

Freud, S. "The Origin and Development of Psychoanalysis", 1910

Freud, S. "Psychopathology of everyday life", 1914

Freud, S. "Beyond the Pleasure Principle", 1920

Frith, C.D. & Dolan, R.J. (1997), 'Abnormal beliefs: Delusions and memory', Paper presented at the May, 1997, Harvard Conference on Memory and Belief.

Gay, Volney, ed. Neuroscience and Religion. Plymouth, UK: Lexington Books, 2009.

Gazzaniga, M. S. (1985). The social brain. New York: Basic Books.

Gazzaniga, M.S. (1993), 'Brain mechanisms and conscious experience', Ciba Foundation Symposium, 174.

Geschwind N. "Behavioural changes in temporal lobe epilepsy". Psychol Med. 1979.

Gellhorn, E., Kiely, W.F. "Mystical states of consciousness: neurophysiological and clinical aspects." J Nerv Ment Dis. 1972;154:399-405.

Gilbert SL, Dobyns WB, Lahn BT (2005) Genetic links between brain development and brain evolution. Nat Rev Genet 6.

Gray JA. The Psychology of Fear and Stress. 2nd ed. New York, NY: Cambridge University Press; 1988.

Gloor, P. (1992), 'Amygdala and temporal lobe epilepsy', in The Amygdala: Neurobiological Aspects of Emotion, Memory and Mental

Dysfunction, ed J.P. Aggleton (New York: Wiley-Liss).

Greenspan, S. I. and S. G. Shanker (2004). The first idea: How symbols, language, and intelligence evolved from our early primate ancestors to modern humans. Cambridge, MA: Da Capo Press.

Grady, D. (1993), 'The vision thing: Mainly in the brain', Discover, June.

Gallagher HL, Frith CD (2003) Functional imaging of 'theory of mind'. Trends Cogn Sci 7: 77.

Gallese V, Fogassi L, Fadiga L, Rizzolatti G (2002) Action representation and the inferior parietal lobule. In: Prinz W, Hommel B (eds) Attention & Performance XIX. Common mechanisms in perception and action. Oxford University Press, Oxford.

Gallese V, Keysers C, Rizzolatti G (2004) A unifying view of the basis of social cognition. Trends Cogn Sci 8: 396–403.

Gangitano M, Mottaghy FM, Pascual-Leone A (2001) Phase specific modulation of cortical motor output during movement observation. NeuroReport 12: 1489–1492.

Gangitano M, Mottaghy FM, Pascual-Leone A (2004) Modulation of premotor mirror neuron activity during observation of unpredictable grasping movements. Eur J Neurosci 20: 2193– 2202.

Goldman AI, Sripada CS (2004) Simulationist models of face-based emotion recognition. Cognition 94: 193–213.

Grèzes J, Costes N, Decety J (1998) Top-down effect of strategy on the perception of human biological motion: a PET investigation. Cogn Neuropsychol 15: 553–582.

Grèzes J, Armony JL, Rowe J, Passingham RE (2003) Activations related to "mirror" and "canonical" neurones in the human brain: an fMRI study. Neuroimage 18: 928–937.

Gross CG, Rocha-Miranda CE, Bender DB (1972) Visual properties of neurons in the inferotemporal cortex of the macaque. J Neurophysiol 35: 96–111.

Hari R, Forss N, Avikainen S, Kirveskari S, Salenius S, Rizzolatti G (1998) Activation of human primary motor cortex during action observation: a neuromagnetic study. Proc. Natl Acad Sci USA 95: 15061–15065.

Hall, Daniel, Keith Meador, and Harold Koenig. "Measuring Religiousness in Health Research: Review and Critique." Journal of Religion and Health 47, no. 2 (2008)

Harris, Sam, Jonas Kaplan, Ashley Curiel, Susan Bookheimer, Marco

Iacoboni, and Mark Cohen. "The Neural Correlates of Religious and Nonreligious Belief." PLoS One 4, no. 10 (October 1, 2009)

Halgren, E. (1992), 'Emotional neurophysiology of the amygdala within the context of human cognition', in The Amygdala: Neurobiological Aspects of Emotion, Memory and Mental Dysfunction, ed J.P. Aggleton (New York: Wiley-Liss).

Halligan PW, Fink GR, Marshal JC, Vallar G. 2003. Spatial cognition: evidence from visual neglect. Trends Cogn Sci.

Handbook of Emotions, Edited by Michael Lewis, Jeannette M. Haviland-Jones, and Lisa Feldman Barrett, The Guilford Press; 3rd edition (2010).

Haggard, P., Clark, S. and Kalogeras,]. (2002) Voluntary action and conscious awareness, Nature Neuroscience 5, 382-5. Haggard, P., Newman, C. and

Magno, E. (1999) On the perceived time of voluntary actions. British Journal of Psychology 90, 291-303.

Hameroff, S.R. and Penrose, R. (1996) Conscious events as orchestrated space-time selections. Journal of Consciousness Studies 3(1), 36-53; also reprinted in J. Shear (ed.) (1997) Explaining Consciousness-The Hard Problem. Cambridge, MA, MIT Press, 177-95.

Hardcastle, V.G. (2000) How to understand theN in NCC. InT. Metzinger (ed.) Neural Correlates of Consciousness. Cambridge, MA, MIT Press, 259-64.

Harding, D.E. (1961) On Having no Head: Zen and the Re-Discovery of the Obvious. London, Buddhist Society.

Hardy, A. (1979) The Spiritual Nature of Man: A Study of Contemporary Religious Experience. Oxford, Clarendon Press.

Hamad, S. (1990) The symbol grounding problem. Physica D 42, 335-46.

Hamad, S. (2001) No easy way out. The Sciences 41(2), 36-42.

Harre, R. and Gillett, G. (1994) The Discursive Mind. Thousand Oaks, CA, Sage.

Haugeland, J. (ed.) (1997) Mind Design II: Philosophy, Psychology, Artificial Intelligence. Cambridge, MA, MIT Press.

Hauser, M.D. (2000) Wild Minds: What Animals Really Think. New York, Henry Holt and Co.; London, Penguin.

Hearne, K. (1990) The Dream Machine. Northants, Aquarian.

Hebb, D.O. (1949) The Organization of Behavior. New York, Wiley.

Helmholtz, H.L.F. von (1856-67) Treatise on Physiological Optics.

Heyes, C.M. (1998) Theory of mind in nonhuman primates. Behavioral and Brain Sciences 21, 101-48; with commentaries.

Heyes, C.M. and Galef, B.G. (eds) (1996) Social Learning in Animals: The Roots of Culture. San Diego, CA, Academic Press.

Hilgard, E.R. (1986) Divided Consciousness: Multiple Controls in Human Thought and Action. New York, Wiley.

Hocquette JF (2016) Is in vitro meat the

solution for the future? Meat Science 120:

167–176

Hodgson, R. (1891) A case of double consciousness. Proceedings of the Society for Psychical Research 7, 221-58.

Hofstadter, D.R. (1979) Code!, Escher, Bach: An Eternal Golden Braid. London, Penguin.

Hofstadter, D.R. and Dennett, D.C. (eds) (1981) The Mind's I: Fantasies and Reflections on Self and Soul. London, Penguin.

Holland, J. (ed.) (2001) Ecstasy: The Complete Guide: A Comprehensive Look at the Risks and Benefits of MDMA. Rochester, VT, Park Street Press.

Holmes, D.S. (1987) The influence of meditation versus rest on physiological arousal. In M. West (ed.) The Psychology of Meditation. Oxford, Clarendon Press, 81-103.

Holt, J. (1999) Blindsight in debates about qualia. Journal of Consciousness Studies 6(5), 54-71.

Horgan, J. (1994), 'Can science explain consciousness?', Scientific American, 271.

Holloway RL (1996) Evolution of the human brain. In: Lock A, Peters CR (eds) Handbook of human symbolic evolution. Oxford University Press, Oxford

Iacoboni M, Woods RP, Brass M, Bekkering H, Mazziotta JC, Rizzolatti G (1999) Cortical mechanisms of human imitation. Science 286: 2526–2528.

Iacoboni M, Koski LM, Brass M, Bekkering H, Woods RP, Dubeau MC, Mazziotta JC, Rizzolatti G (2001) Reafferent copies of imitated actions in the right superior temporal cortex. Proc Natl Acad Sci USA 98: 13995–13999.

Jeannerod M (1988) The neural and behavioural organization of goal-directed movements. Clarendon Press, Oxford.

Johnson-Frey SH, Maloof FR, Newman-Norlund R, Farrer C, Inati S,

Grafton ST (2003) Actions or hand-objects interactions? Human inferior frontal cortex and action observation. Neuron 39: 1053–1058.

Jackson, F. (1982) Epiphenomenal qualia. Philosophical Quarterly 32, 127-36.

James, W. (1890) The Principles of Psychology (2 volumes). London, Macmillan.

James, W. (1902) The Varieties of Religious Experience: A Study in Human Nature. New York and London, Longmans, Green and Co.

Jansen, K. (2001) Ketamine: Dreams and Realities. Sarasota, FL, Multidisciplinary Association for Psychedelic Studies.

Jay, M. (ed.) (1999) Artificial Paradises: A Drugs Reader. London, Penguin.

Jaynes, J. (1976) The Origin of Consciousness in the Breakdown of the Bicameral Mind. New York, Houghton Mifflin.

Johnson, M.K. and Raye, C.L. (1981) Reality monitoring. Psychological Review 88, 67-85.

Kadim I, Mahgoub O, Baqir S et al. (2015) Cultured meat from muscle stem cells: a review of challenges and prospects. J Integr Agr 14: 222–233

Koski L, Iacoboni M, Dubeau MC, Woods RP, Mazziotta JC (2003) Modulation of cortical activity during different imitative behaviors. J Neurophysiol 89: 460–471.

Krolak-Salmon P, Henaff MA, Isnard J, Tallon-Baudry C, Guenot M, Vighetto A, Bertrand O, Mauguiere F (2003) An attention modulated response to disgust in human ventral anterior insula. Ann Neurol 53: 446–453.

Kandel, E. R. In Search of Memory: The Emergence of a New Science of

Mind, W. W. Norton & Company (2007).

Kandel E. R. Schwartz JH, Jessel TM. Principles of neural sciences. New York; McGraw Hill, 2000.

Kanizsa, G. (1979), Organization In Vision (New York: Praeger).

Kaloupek DG, Scott JR, Khatami V. Assessment of coping strategies associated with syncope in blood donors. J Psychosom Res. 1985;29:207-214.

Kanwisher, N. (2001) Neural events and perceptual awareness. Cognition 79, 89-113; also reprinted inS. Dehaene (ed.) The Cognitive Neuroscience of Consciousness. Cambridge, MA, MIT Press, 89-113.

Kapleau, Roshi P. (1980) The Three Pillars of Zen: Teaching, Practice, and Enlightenment (revised edn). New York, Doubleday.

Karn, K. and Hayhoe, M. (2000) Memory representations guide targeting eye movements in a natural task. Visual Cognition 7, 673-703.

Kasamatsu, A. and Hirai, T. (1966) An electroencephalographic study on the Zen meditation (zazen). Folia Psychiatrica et Neurologica Japonica 20, 315-36.

Kaiserman-Abramof, I. R., Graybiel, A. M., & Nauta, W. J. (1980). The thalamic projection to cortical area 17 in a congenitally anophthalmic mouse strain. Neuroscience, 5, 41–52.

Kanold, P. O., Kara, P., Reid, R. C., & Shatz, C. J. (2003). Role of subplate neurons in functional maturation of visual cortical columns. Science, 301, 521–525.

Kennedy, H., & Dehay, C. (1988). Functional implications of the anatomical organization of the callosal projections of visual areas V1 and V2 in the macaque monkey. Behav. Brain Res., 29, 225–236.

Kennedy, H., & Dehay, C. (1993). Cortical specifi cation of mice and men. Cereb. Cortex, 3, 171–186.

Kentridge, R.W. and Heywood, C.A. (1999) The status of blindsight. Journal of Consciousness Studies 6(5), 3-11.

Kihlstrom, J.F. (1996) Perception without awareness of what is perceived, learning without awareness of what is learned. In M. Velmans (ed.) The Science of Consciousness. London, Routledge, 23-46.

Kluver, H. (1926) Mescal visions and eidetic vision. American Journal of Psychology 37, 502-15.

Kollerstrom, N. (1999) The path of Halley's comet, and Newton's late apprehension of the law of gravity. Annals of Science 56, 331-56.

Kosslyn, S.M. (1980) Image and Mind. Cambridge, MA, Harvard University Press.

Kosslyn, S.M. (1988) Aspects of a cognitive neuroscience of mental imagery. Science 240, 1621-6.

Kinsbourne, M. (1995), 'The intralaminar thalamic nucleii', Consciousness and Cognition, 4.

Kjaer, Troels, Camilla Bertelsen, Paola Piccini, David Brooks, Jorgen Alving, and Hans Lou. "Increased Dopamine Tone during Meditation- Induced Change of Consciousness." Cognitive Brain Research 13, no. 2 (April 2002)

Kölmel HW. 1985. Complex visual hallucinations in the hemianopic field. J Neurol Neurosurg Psychiatry.

Koenig, Harold. "Research on Religion, Spirituality, and Mental Health: A Review." Canadian Journal of Psychiatry 54, no. 5 (May 2009)

Koenig, Harold, ed. Handbook of Religion and Mental Health. San Diego, CA: Academic Press, 1998

Kraepelin E. Psychiatry: A Textbook for Students and Physicians. New York, NY: Science History Publications; 1990.

Lauglin, Charles, John McManus, and Eugene d'Aquili. Brain, Symbol, and Experience. 2nd ed. New York: Columbia University Press, 1992

Lakoff, G. and M. Johnson (1999). Philosophy in the flesh. Basic Books: New York.

LeDoux, J. E. (1996). The emotional brain. New York: Simon & Schuster.

LeDoux, J.E. (1992), 'Emotion and the amygdala', in The Amygdala: Neurobiological Aspects of Emo- tion, Memory and Mental Dysfunction, ed J.P. Aggleton (New York: Wiley-Liss).

Levin, D.T. and Simons, D.J. (1997) Failure to detect changes to attended objects in motion pictures. Psychonomic Bulletin and Review 4, 501-6.

Levine,J. (1983) Materialism and qualia: the explanatory gap. Pacific Philosophical Quarterly 64, 354-61.

Levine,J. (2001) Purple Haze: The Puzzle of Consciousness. New York, Oxford University Press. Levine, S. (1979) A Gradual Awakening. New York, Doubleday.

Levinson, B.W. (1965) States of awareness during general anaesthesia. British Journal of Anaesthesia 37, 544-6.

Lewicki, P., Czyzewska, M. and Hoffman, H. (1987) Unconscious acquisition of complex procedural knowledge. Journal of Experimental Psychology: Learning, Memory and Cognition 13, 523-30.

Lewicki, P., Hill, T. and Bizot, E. (1988) Acquisition of procedural knowledge about a pattern of stimuli that cannot be articulated. Cognitive Psychology 20, 24-37.

Lewicki, P., Hill, T. and Czyzewska, M. (1992) Nonconscious acquisition of information. American Psychologist 47, 796-801.

Manthey S, Schubotz RI, von Cramon DY (2003). Premotor cortex in observing erroneous action: an fMRI study. Brain Res Cogn Brain Res 15: 296–307.

M. Colombo, "Why build a virtual brain? Large-scale neural simulations as jump start for cognitive computing," Journal of Experimental and Theoretical Artificial Intelligence, vol. 29, pp. 361-370, 2017.

Mesulam MM, Mufson EJ (1982) Insula of the old world monkey. III: Efferent cortical output and comments on function. J Comp Neurol 212: 38–52.

Naskar, Abhijit. "Love Sutra: The Neuroscientific Manual of Love", 2015

Naskar, Abhijit. "What is Mind?", 2016

Naskar, Abhijit. "In Search of Divinity: Journey to The Kingdom of Conscience", 2016

Naskar, Abhijit. "Love, God & Neurons: Memoir of A Scientist who found himself by getting lost", 2016

Naskar, Abhijit. "Neurons of Jesus: Mind of A Teacher, Spouse & Thinker", 2017

Naskar, Abhijit. "Rowdy Buddha: The First Sapiens", 2017

Naskar, Abhijit. "The Education Decree", 2017

Naskar, Abhijit. "Principia Humanitas", 2017

Naskar, Abhijit. "We Are All Black: A Treatise on Racism", 2017

Naskar, Abhijit. "Wise Mating: A Treatise on Monogamy", 2017

Naskar, Abhijit. "The Bengal Tigress: A Treatise on Gender Equality", 2017

Naskar, Abhijit. "I Am The Thread: My Mission", 2017

Naskar, Abhijit. "Morality Absolute", 2017

Naskar, Abhijit. "Fabric of Humanity", 2018

Naskar, Abhijit. "The Constitution of The United Peoples of Earth", 2019

Naskar, Abhijit. "When Humans Unite: Making A World Without Borders", 2019

Naskar, Abhijit. "Mission Reality", 2019

Naskar, Abhijit. "Citizens of Peace: Beyond The Savagery of Sovereignty", 2019

Naskar, Abhijit. "Neurons Giveth, Neurons Taketh Away | Abhijit Naskar | TEDxIIMRanchi", 2019

https://www.youtube.com/watch?v=B
NX-Q0ySm80

Newberg, Andrew, and Jeremy Iversen. "The Neural Basis of the Complex Mental Task of Meditation: Neurotransmitter and Neurochemical Considerations." Medical Hypotheses 61, no. 2 (2003).

Newberg, Andrew. "How God Changes Your Brain: An Introduction to Jewish Neurotheology", CCAR Journal: The Reform Jewish Quarterly, Winter 2016.

Newberg, Andrew, and Stephanie Newberg. "A Neuropsychological Perspective on Spiritual Development." In Handbook of Spiritual Development in Childhood and Adolescence, edited by Eugene Roehlkepartain, Pamela King, Linda Wagener, and Peter Benson. London: Sage Publications, Inc., 2005

Newberg, Andrew. "The Neurotheology Link An Intersection Between Spirituality and Health", Alternative and Complimentary Therapies, Vol 21 No 1, February 2015.

Newberg, Andrew, Nancy Wintering, Dharma Khalsa, Hannah Roggenkamp, and Mark Waldman. "Meditation Effects on Cognitive Function and Cerebral Blood Flow in Subjects with Memory Loss: A Preliminary Study." Journal of Alzheimer's Disease 20, no. 2 (2010)

Nash, M. (1995), 'Glimpses of the mind', Time.

Nesse RM. Proximate and evolutionary studies of anxiety, stress and depression: synergy at the interface. Neurosci Biobehav Rev. 1999;23:895-903.

Nishitani N, Hari R (2000) Temporal dynamics of cortical representation for action. Proc Natl Acad Sci USA 97: 913–918.

Nishitani N, Hari R (2002) Viewing lip forms: cortical dynamics. Neuron 36: 1211–1220.

O'Hara, K. and Scutt, T. (1996) There is no hard problem of consciousness. Journal of Consciousness Studies 3(4), 290-302, reprinted in J. Shear (ed.) (1997) Explaining Consciousness. Cambridge, MA, MIT Press, 69-82.

O'Regan, J.K. (1992) Solving the "real" mysteries of visual perception: the world as an outside memory. Canadian Journal of Psychology 46, 461-88.

O'Regan, J.K. and Noe, A. (2001) A sensorimotor account of vision and visual consciousness. Behavioral and Brain Sciences 24(5), 883-917.

O'Regan, J.K., Rensink, R.A. and Clark,].]. (1999) Change-blindness as a result of "mudsplashes." Nature 398, 34.

Ornstein, R.E. (1977) The Psychology of Consciousness (2nd edn). New York, Harcourt.

Ornstein, R.E. (1986) The Psychology of Consciousness (3rd edn). New York, Pehguin.

Ornstein, R.E. (1992) The Evolution of Consciousness. New York, Touchstone.

Penfield W, Faulk ME (1955) The insula: further observations on its function. Brain 78: 445– 470.

Penrose, R. (1994), Shadows of the Mind (Oxford: Oxford University Press).

Penrose, R. (1989), The Emperor's New Mind: Concerning Computers, Minds and The Laws of Physics (Oxford: Oxford University Press).

Persinger, "'I would kill in God's name' role of sex, weekly church attendance, report of a religious experience and limbic lability" Perceptual and Motor Skills 1997.

Persinger "Experimental simulation of the God experience" Neurotheology 2003.

Persinger, M. A. (1993b). Personality changes following brain injury as a grief response to the loss of sense of self: Phenomenological themes as indices of local lability and neurocognitive restructuring as psycho- therapy. Psychological Reports, 72

Persinger, Corradini, Clement, Keaney, et al "Neurotheology and its convergence with neuroquantology" NeuroQuantology 2010.

Persinger, Koren and St-Pierre "The electromagnetic induction of mystical and altered states within the laboratory" Journal of Consciousness Exploration and Research 2010.

Persinger "Case report: A prototypical spontaneous 'sensed presence' of a sentient being and concomitant electroencephalographic activity in the clinical laboratory" Neurocase 2008.

Persinger and Saroka "Potential production of Hughlings Jackson's "parasitic consciousness" by physiologically-patterned weak transcerebral magnetic fields: QEEG and source localization" Epilepsy & Behavior 28 (2013).

Persinger. "The neuropsychiatry of paranormal experiences". J Neuropsychiatry Clin Neurosci 2001.

Persinger. "Neuropsychological bases of god beliefs", New York: Praeger, 1987

Persinger. "Temporal lobe epileptic signs and correlative behaviors

displayed by normal populations",
Journal of General Psychology, 1986

Persinger "Experimental Facilitation of the Sensed Presence: Possible Intercalation between the Hemispheres Induced by Complex Magnetic Fields" Journal of Nervous and Mental Disease 2002.

Palmer J. 1978. The out-of-body experience: a psychological theory. Parapsychol Rev.

Page AC. Blood-injury phobia. Clinical Psychology Review. 1994;14:443-461.

Perry BD, Pollard R. Homeostasis, stress, trauma, and adaptation. A neurodevelopmental view of childhood trauma. Child Adolesc Psychiatr Clin N Am. 1998;7:33.

Paré, D. & Llinás, R. (1995), 'Conscious and preconscious processes as seen from the standpoint of sleep-waking cycle neurophysiology', Neuropsychologia, 33.

P. S. de Laplace. Essai Philosophique sur les Probabilites [1814], in Academy des Sciences, Oeuvres Complotes de Laplace, Vol. 7, Gauthier-Villars, Paris (1886).

Perrett DI, Harries MH, Bevan R, Thomas S, Benson PJ, Mistlin AJ, Chitty AJ, Hietanen JK, Ortega JE (1989) Frameworks of analysis for the neural representation of animate objects and actions. J Exp Bio 146: 87–113.

Phillips ML, Young AW, Senior C, Brammer M, Andrew C, Calder AJ, Bullmore ET, Perrett DI, Rowland D, Williams SC, Gray JA, David AS (1997) A specific neural substrate for perceiving facial expressions of disgust. Nature 389: 495–498.

Phillips ML, Young AW, Scott SK, Calder AJ, Andrew C, Giampietro V, Williams SC, Bullmore ET, Brammer M, Gray JA (1998) Neural responses to facial and vocal expressions of fear and disgust. Proc R Soc Lond B Biol Sci 265: 1809–1817.

Puce A, Perrett D (2003) Electrophysiological and brain imaging of biological motion. Philosoph Trans Royal Soc Lond, Series B, 358: 435–445.

Ramachandran VS. Behavioral and magnetoencephalographic correlates of plasticity in the adult human brain. Proc Natl Acad Sci USA 1993; 90: 10413–20.

Ramachandran VS. Phantom limbs, neglect syndromes, repressed memories, and Freudian psychology. Int Rev Neurobiol 1994; 37: 291–333.

Ramachandran VS. Plasticity and functional recovery in neurology. Clin Med 2005; 5: 368–73.

Ramachandran VS, Hirstein W. The perception of phantom limbs. The D. O. Hebb lecture. Brain 1998; 121: 1603–30.

Ramachandran VS, McGeoch PD, Williams L, Arcilla G. Rapid relief of thalamic pain syndrome induced by vestibular caloric stimulation. Neurocase 2007; 13: 185–8.

Ramachandran VS, Rogers-Ramachandran D, Cobb S. Touching the phantom limb. Nature 1995; 377: 489–90.

Ramachandran VS, Rogers-Ramachandran D. Phantom limbs and neural plasticity. Arch Neurol 2000; 57: 317–20.

Ramachandran VS, Rogers-Ramachandran D. It's all done with mirrors. Sci Am Mind 2007; 18: 16–9.

Ramachandran VS, Rogers-Ramachandran D. Sensations referred to a patient's phantom arm from another subjects intact arm: perceptual correlates of mirror neurons. Med Hypotheses 2008; 70: 1233–4.

Ramachandran VS, Rogers-Ramachandran D, Stewart M. Perceptual correlates of massive cortical reorganization. Science 1992; 258: 1159–60.

Rizzolatti G, Craighero L (2004) The mirror-neuron system. Annu Rev Neurosci 27: 169–192.

Rizzolatti G, Scandolara C, Matelli M, Gentilucci M (1981) Afferent properties of periarcuate neurons in macaque monkeys. I. Somatosensory responses. Behav Brain Res 2: 125–146.

Rizzolatti G, Fadiga L, Matelli M, Bettinardi V, Paulesu E, Perani D, Fazio F (1996) Localization of grasp representation in humans by PET: 1. Observation versus execution. Exp Brain Res 111: 246–252.

Rizzolatti G, Fogassi L, Gallese V (2001) Neurophysiological mechanisms underlying the understanding and imitation of action. Nature Rev Neurosci 2:661–670.

Rock I, Victor J. Vision and touch: an experimentally created conflict between the two senses. Science 1964; 143: 594–6.

Rose'n B, Lundborg G. Training with a mirror in rehabilitation of the hand. Scand J Plast Reconstr Surg Hand Surg 2005; 39: 104–8.

Royet JP, Plailly J, Delon-Martin C, Kareken DA, Segebarth C (2003) fMRI of emotional responses to odors: influence of hedonic valence and judgment, handedness, and gender. Neuroimage 20: 713–728.

Rozin R Haidt J and McCauley CR (2000) Disgust. In: Lewis M, Haviland-Jones JM (eds) Handbook of Emotion. 2nd Edition. Guilford Press, New York, pp 637–653.

Saxe R, Carey S, Kanwisher N (2004) Understanding other minds: linking developmental psychology and functional neuroimaging. Annu Rev Psychol 55: 87–124.

S. J. Russell and P. Norvig, Artificial intelligence: a modern approach (3rd edition): Prentice Hall, 2009.

Schienle A, Stark R, Walter B, Blecker C, Ott U, Kirsch P, Sammer G, Vaitl D (2002) The insula is not specifically involved in disgust processing: an fMRI study. Neuroreport 13: 2023–2026.

Showers MJC, Lauer EW (1961) Somatovisceral motor patterns in the insula. J Comp Neurol 117: 107–115.

Singer T, Seymour B, O'Doherty J, Kaube H, Dolan RJ, Frith CD (2004) Empathy for pain involves the affective but not the sensory components of pain. Science 303: 1157–1162.

Small DM, Gregory MD, Mak YE, Gitelman D, Mesulam MM, Parrish T

(2003) Dissociation of neural representation of intensity and affective valuation in human gustation Neuron 39: 701–711.

Smith A (1759) The theory of moral sentiments (ed. 1976). Clarendon Press, Oxford.

Sprengelmeyer R, Rausch M, Eysel UT, Przuntek H (1998) Neural structures associated with recognition of facial expressions of basic emotions Proc R Soc Lond B Biol Sci 265: 1927–1931.

Strafella AP, Paus T (2000) Modulation of cortical excitability during action observation: a transcranial magnetic stimulation study. NeuroReport 11: 2289–2292.

Simonsen R (2015) Eating for the future: veganism and the challenge of in vitro meat. In: Stapleton P, Byers A (Hg). Biopolitics and utopia. Palgrave Macmillan, New York (2015), S 167–190

Tanaka K (1996) Inferotemporal cortex and object vision. Ann Rev Neurosci. 19: 109–140.

T. R. Society, "Machine learning: the power and promise of computers that learn by example," ed. The Royal Society, 2017.

Tomasello M, Call J (1997) Primate cognition. Oxford University Press, Oxford.

Tremblay C, Robert M, Pascual-Leone A, Lepore F, Nguyen DK, Carmant L, Bouthillier A, Theoret H (2004) Action observation and execution: intracranial recordings in a human subject. Neurology. 63: 937–938.

Umilta MA, Kohler E, Gallese V, Fogassi L, Fadiga L, Keysers C, Rizzolatti G (2001) "I know what you are doing": a neurophysiological study. Neuron 32: 91–101.

Von Wright G.H., (1963), Norm and Action. A Logical Inquiry, Routledge & Kegan Paul, London.

Von Wright G.H., (1976), "Determinism and the Study of Man", in Essays on Explanation and Understanding, ed. by J. Manninen and R. Tuomela, Reidel, Dordrecht.

Von Wright G.H., (1977), "What is Humanism?", The Lindlay Lecture, University of Arkansas, Lawrence, Kansas.

Von Wright G.H., (1979), "Humanism and the Humanities", in Philosophy and Grammar, ed. by S. Kanger and S. Öhman, Reidel, Dordrecht, pp. 1-16. Reprinted in von Wright (1993).

Von Wright G.H., (1980), Freedom and Determination, North-Holland Publishing Co., Amsterdam.

Von Wright G.H., (1985), Of Human Freedom, The Tanner Lectures on Human Values,

Vol. VI, ed. by S. M. McMurrin, University of Utah Press, Salt Lake City, pp. 107-70. Reprinted in von Wright (1998).

Von Wright G.H., (1993), The Tree of Knowledge and Other Essays, Brill, Leiden.

Von Wright G.H., (1997), "Progress: Fact and Fiction", in The Idea of Progress, ed. by A. Burgen et al., W. de Gruyter, Berlin, pp. 1-18.

Von Wright G.H., (1998), In the Shadow of Descartes: Essays in the Philosophy of Mind, Kluwer, Dordrecht.

Visalberghi E, Fragaszy D. (2002). Do monkeys ape? Ten years after. In: Dautenhahn K, Nehaniv C (eds) Imitation in animals and artifacts. MIT Press, Boston. Pp. 471–500

Weele C, Driessen C. (2016) In vitro meat is a chance to rethink. In: Stephens N, Kramer C, Denfeld Z,

Strand R (Hg). What is in vitro meat? Food Phreaking Issue 02: 57–59

Wicker B, Keysers C, Plailly J, Royet JP, Gallese V, Rizzolatti G (2003) Both of us disgusted in my insula: the common neural basis of seeing and feeling disgust. Neuron 40: 655–664.

Yokochi H, Tanaka M, Kumashiro M, Iriki A (2003) Inferior parietal somatosensory neurons coding face-hand coordination in Japanese macaques. Somatosens Mot Res 20 : 115–125.

Zald DH, Pardo JV (2000) Functional neuroimaging of the olfactory system in humans. Int J Psychophysiol 36: 165–181.

Zald DH, Donndelinger MJ, Pardo JV (1998) Elucidating dynamic brain interactions with across-subjects correlational analyses of positron emission tomographic data: the functional connectivity of the amygdala and orbitofrontal cortex during olfactory tasks. J Cereb Blood Flow Metab 18: 896–905.

SEE NO GENDER

SEE NO GENDER

www.ingramcontent.com/pod-product-compliance
Lightning Source LLC
Chambersburg PA
CBHW031231250726
48655CB00005B/1903